Curious Questions & Answers about...

Science

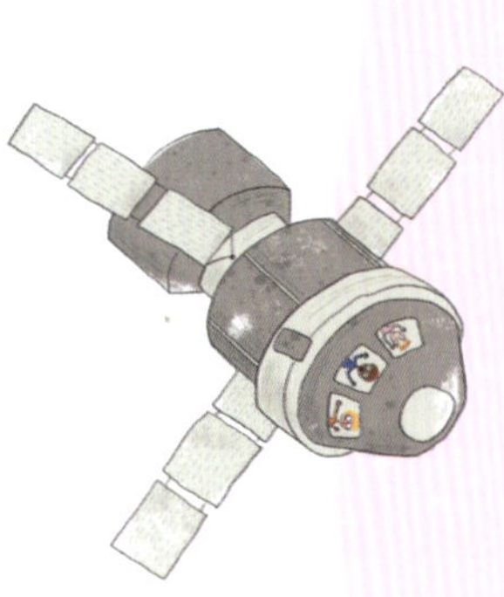

First published in 2018 by Miles Kelly Publishing Ltd
Harding's Barn, Bardfield End Green, Thaxted, Essex, CM6 3PX, UK
Unit 5A The Court, Ashbourne Industrial Estate, Ashbourne,
Co. Meath, A84 DP73, Eire

Copyright © Miles Kelly Publishing Ltd 2018

2 4 6 8 10 9 7 5 3 1

Publishing Director Belinda Gallagher
Creative Director Jo Cowan
Editorial Director Rosie Neave
Senior Editor Amy Johnson
Senior Designer Rob Hale
Cover Designers Andrea Slane, Mark Penfound
Image Manager Liberty Newton
Production Elizabeth Collins
Reprographics Stephan Davis
Assets Venita Kidwai

ISBN 978-1-83515-099-3

Printed in China

British Library Cataloguing-in-Publication Data
A catalogue record for this book is available from the British Library

Made with paper from a sustainable forest

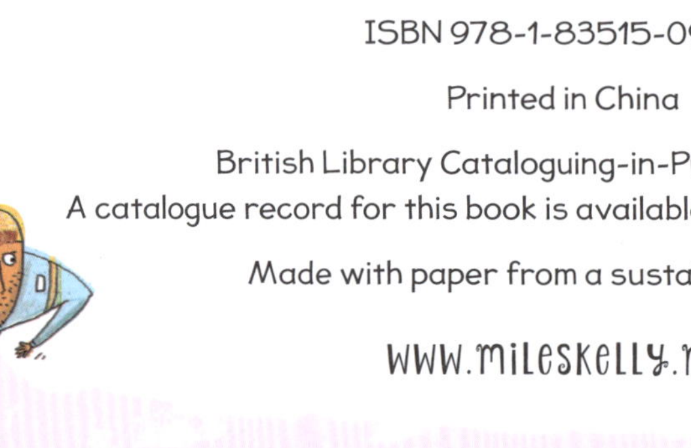

www.mileskelly.net

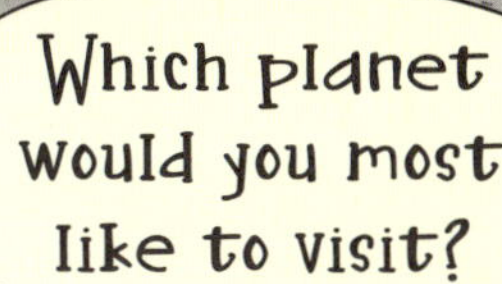

Curious Questions & Answers about...

Science

Words by Anne Rooney

Illustrations by Pauline Gregory

MILES KELLY

How do we find things out?

We know about the world around us because scientists look carefully and carry out experiments. You could be a scientist! All you have to do is...

① **Spot a problem**
Keep your eyes and ears open. Look out for questions to ask and problems to solve.

② **Have an idea**
Think of something that could explain or solve the problem. This is your theory.

③ **Design an experiment**
Work out how to test your idea – an experiment. Change just one thing at a time to make a fair test.

④ **Check what happens**
Were you right? If not, you might need a new theory and a new experiment.

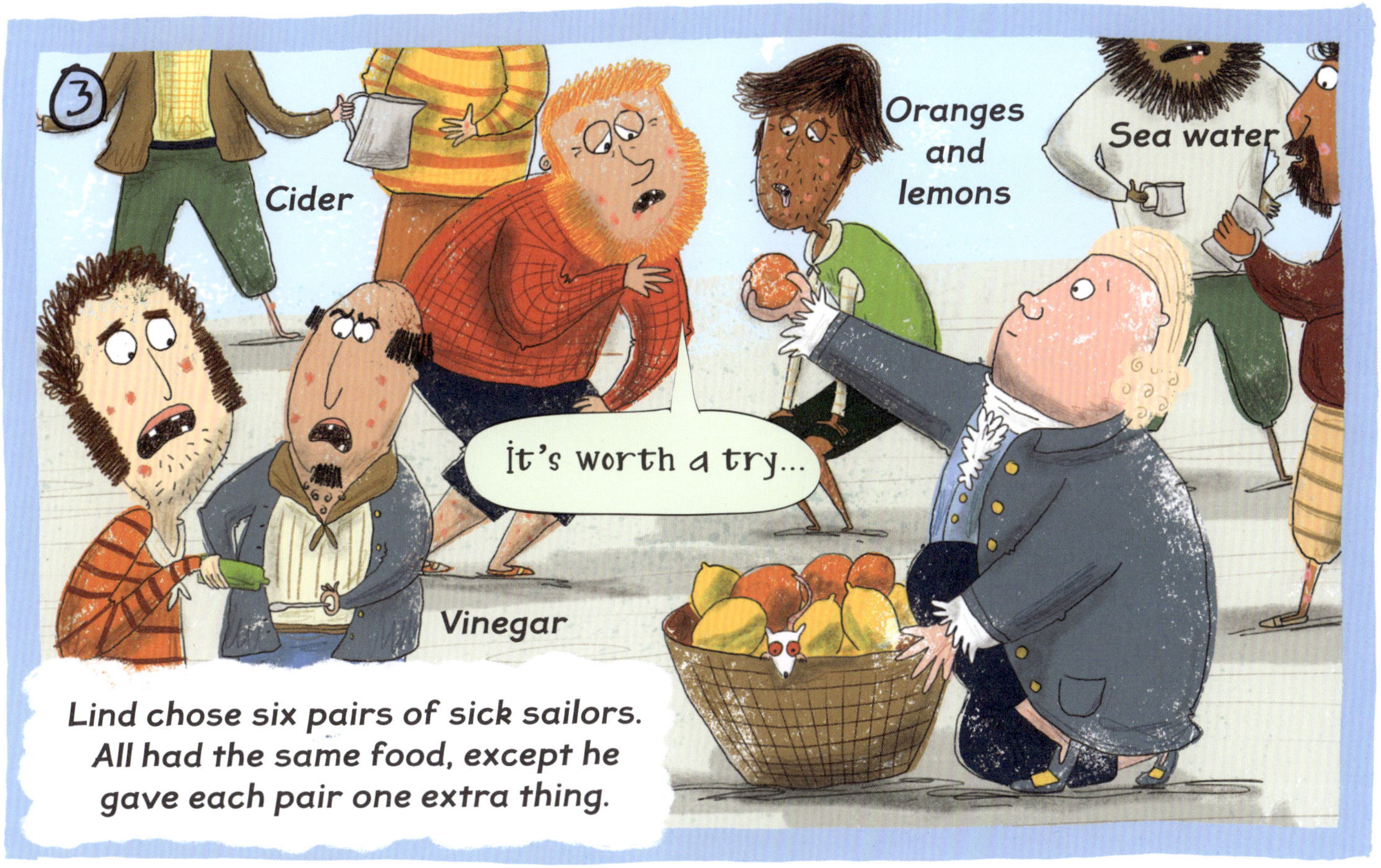

Lind chose six pairs of sick sailors. All had the same food, except he gave each pair one extra thing.

Why do we need scientists?

The work of scientists can make life better. A discovery can lead to more questions and experiments. Science keeps on going.

Modern scientists found out that it is the Vitamin C in fruit that stops scurvy.

Do plants eat?

Plants don't eat like animals do – they use sunlight to make their own food in their leaves.

What use are roots?

Roots keep plants fixed in the soil so they don't fall over or blow away! Through their roots, plants take in water and small amounts of chemicals from the soil. Roots also store food for the plant.

How are new plants made?

Most plants reproduce – make baby plants – by producing seeds.

The seeds fall to the ground, blow away in the wind, or are spread by animals to new places to grow.

Some plants make fruit with seeds in. Animals eat the fruit. The seeds come out in their poo, ready to grow somewhere else.

Certain types of plants grow baby plants on special stalks called runners. The new plants then grow their own roots and the runner drops off.

How many?

320

The number of days it would take to drive to the Moon non-stop at 50 kilometres per hour.

60–70

The percentage of your body that is water.

300,000,000

The speed in metres per second that light travels.

3%

How much taller an astronaut is in space where gravity is not pulling their body downwards.

50%

The proportion of cells in your body that are not you, but germs and other micro organisms.

A skydiver can reach a speed of **195** kilometres per hour.

1,000,000,000,000,000,000,000,000

Roughly how many stars there are in the known Universe.

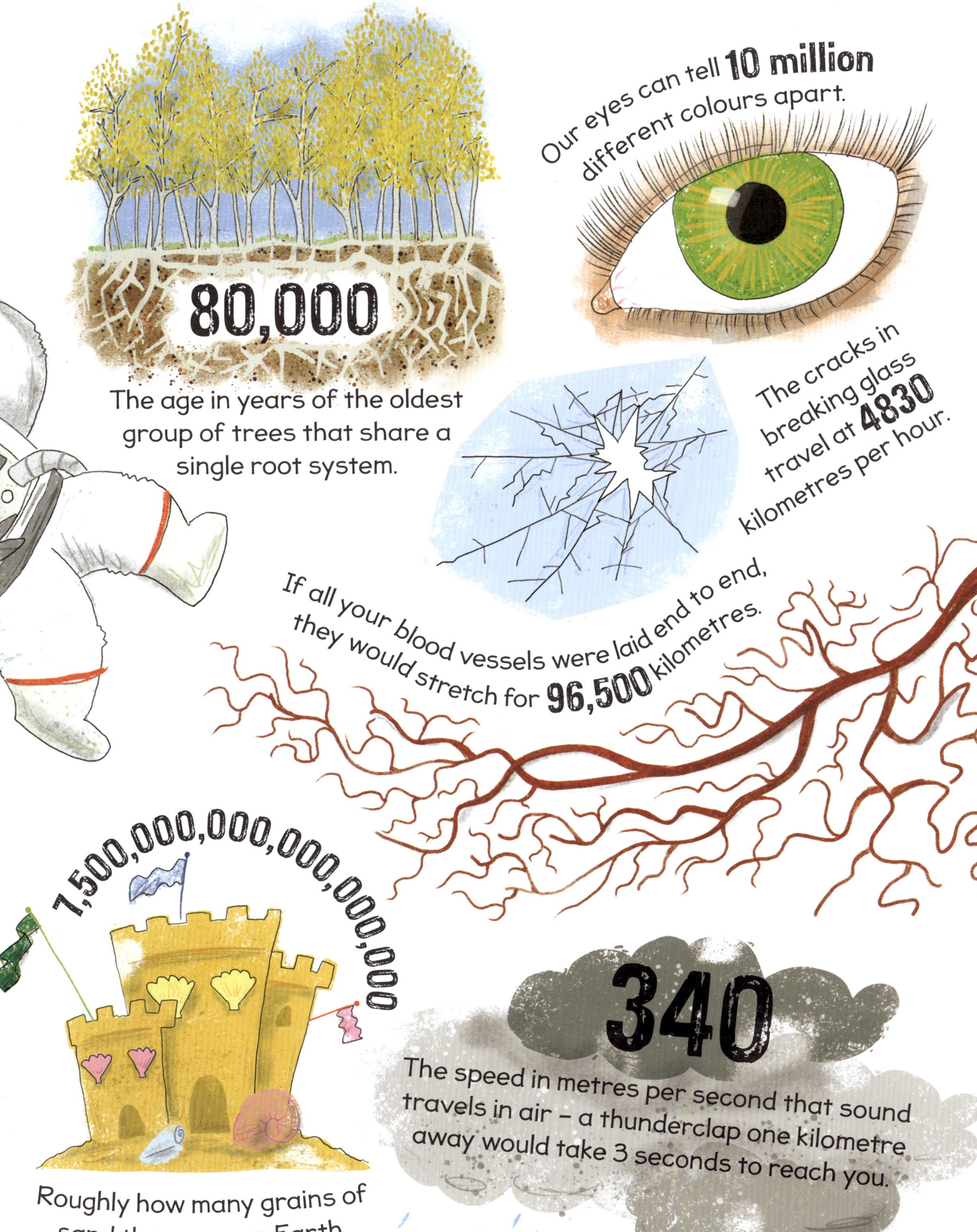

80,000

The age in years of the oldest group of trees that share a single root system.

Our eyes can tell **10 million** different colours apart.

The cracks in breaking glass travel at **4830** kilometres per hour.

If all your blood vessels were laid end to end, they would stretch for **96,500** kilometres.

7,500,000,000,000,000,000

Roughly how many grains of sand there are on Earth.

340

The speed in metres per second that sound travels in air – a thunderclap one kilometre away would take 3 seconds to reach you.

What can you hear in space?

Nothing, there are no sounds in space. Sound travels as vibrations through matter. As space is empty, there is nothing for sound to travel through.

Why do things sound different underwater?

The vibrations are going through water, not air, making things sound a bit different. We can hear higher sounds in water than in air.

Do we all hear the same sounds?

No – children can hear higher and lower sounds than grown-ups. You can probably hear bats squeaking and high-pitched dog whistles, when older people hear nothing.

What's the loudest sound ever?

A volcano called Krakatau erupted in Indonesia in 1883, making the loudest sound humans have ever heard. It could be heard 5000 kilometres away.

How does electricity get to my house?

Electricity is a type of energy. It is generated in power stations then carried along a network of cables, all the way to the wires and power points throughout your house.

How is electricity made?

We get electricity by changing other forms of energy such as sunlight, wind, moving water, or by burning coal, oil or gas.

Coal, oil and gas are known as fossil fuels, because they come from the remains of animals and plants that lived long ago. A lot of our energy comes from burning fossil fuels.

Wires inside the walls carry electricity to all the places it's needed. We plug electrical objects into sockets in the wall.

Fossil fuels will run out in the future, and burning them causes pollution. So people are trying to use more energy from sources that can't be used up.

Solar power

Energy from sunlight is captured in solar panels and changed into electricity.

Water power

The energy of water held by a dam is changed into electrical energy.

Wind power

Wind turbines change the wind's movement energy into electricity.

Why do I feel ill?

Many illnesses are caused by germs – tiny things too small to see. There are germs everywhere. Your body tries to keep them out, and is good at fighting them when they get in.

How does my body fight germs?

It makes special cells (tiny parts of your body) that attack germs and anything else that shouldn't be inside you.

1. Once inside your body, germs set up home and start reproducing – soon there are lots and lots.

2. Special body cells come to the rescue by attacking the germs.

3. They destroy the germs by swallowing them whole!

What is a fever?

You might feel hot when you're ill. Your body pushes its temperature up to kill off germs that don't like the heat. This doesn't feel good, but it does you good!

Can I get the same type of germ again?

When you catch an illness like chickenpox, your body learns how to fight it. You probably won't get it again: if another chickenpox germ comes along, your body can deal with it quickly — it doesn't stand a chance.

Did you know?

Some **plants** eat insects and even small animals.

There are **meteorites** – tiny bits of rock from space – all around. One hits each square metre of ground about once a year.

If you break a **magnet** in half, you get two magnets, each with a north and south pole.

If we could drill a hole right through the **Earth**, things wouldn't fall straight through; they would get to the middle and stop.

Nine tenths of an **iceberg** is under water. Ice only just floats, so not much sticks out.

If you put a **carnation** in coloured water, it will eventually suck up the water and turn the same colour.

Bamboo grows so fast you can watch it get taller. It can grow 91 centimetres in a single day.

If there was no air, a **feather** and **cricket ball** dropped from the same height would hit the ground together.

The **Apollo spacecraft** were landed on the Moon by a computer less powerful than a smartphone.

The largest land animal ever was **Patagotitan**, a dinosaur that weighed about 70 tonnes and was 37 metres long.

Some **volcanic rocks** float on water. This is because they are full of air bubbles.

If you float a **needle** on water it lines up to point north/south.

Earth's continents move slowly all the time, so the **Atlantic Ocean** grows a few centimetres wider each year.

Why do I have a shadow?

Your body blocks light coming from the Sun or a lamp, making a darker patch on the other side.

Why is my reflection the wrong way round?

Light from the left side of your body travels to the mirror and bounces off, making the left side of your reflection.

What makes a rainbow?

If sunlight (white light) passes through raindrops at the right angle, it is split up into a spectrum of colours inside the raindrops. The colours come out in different directions.

You see one colour from each raindrop – which colour depends on the angle you are looking at the raindrop. All together they make stripes – a rainbow!

Why can't I see round corners?

Light always travels in straight lines. You can see round corners, but only if you bounce the light around a bit using mirrors. This is how a periscope in a submarine works.

What eats lions?

A few things nibble lions – like biting insects – and crocodiles sometimes kill lions. But mostly lions eat other animals. The world is full of creatures that eat each other.

How do animals make a chain?

The order in which animals eat each other – and plants – is called a food chain. It's easy to see who eats who.

An omnivore is an animal that is able to eat both plants and other animals. Are you a carnivore, herbivore or omnivore?

Whose food is already dead?

Some creatures, such as vultures, eat carrion — animals that have already died. Vultures will eat the dead lion one day — and so will tiny bugs and worms.

What is a carnivore?

Carnivores are animals that eat other animals. Lions eat zebras, antelope and sometimes young giraffes.

Which animals help hippos?

These oxpeckers help me by eating the insects that bite my skin. This helps them because they get a good meal!

Why do things fall?

The force of gravity pulls objects towards the centre of the Earth – downwards! Gravity is everywhere in the Universe, pulling things with less mass towards things with more mass. The Earth has more mass than anything on it.

Why does a parachute slow your fall?

A force called drag acts on the parachute. When the parachute opens, air is trapped under it. The air has to be pushed out of the way for the parachute to fall. The air holds the parachute up while gravity pulls it down.

How does a magnet stick your picture to the fridge?

Some metals are magnetic (they will stick to a magnet). Magnetism is a force that can act even through thin layers that are not magnetic — like paper.

Which force stops you slipping?

Friction is a force between surfaces that stops them sliding over each other. On ice, there is very little friction. There is more between rough surfaces, so your shoes grip to a rough road surface and slip on ice.

Would you rather?

Would you rather be a **vulture** that eats dead animals or a **worm** that eats soil?

If you were a superhero, would you rather have enough **friction** to walk up walls or be able to turn **gravity** off and float around?

Would it be better to be able to see **round corners** or in the **dark**?

Would you prefer to study **tigers** in the jungle or explore scary **volcanoes**?

Would you rather invent an amazing new **material** or design a fantastic **vehicle**?

Would you rather be **super-stretchy** like elastic, or **super-springy** and bounce everywhere?

Time for adventure! Would you rather be an **astronaut** going to Mars or a **diver** exploring the deepest oceans?

Would you rather be so **light** you can walk on water...

...or so **dense** you could walk along the seabed?

Which force pushes up?

Buoyancy! Buoyancy is a force that pushes upwards through a fluid (such as water or air) against the weight of an object. When the weight pushing down (gravity) and the buoyancy are equal, the object doesn't move up or down.

Why do ships float?

Whether something sinks or floats depends on its density (how heavy something is for its volume). Most big ships are made of metal. Metal is more dense than water, but a ship floats because it is mostly full of air.

Do fish sink or float?

They can do both! Fish are almost the same density as water. Many types have a swim bladder, which is a sac filled with gas in their stomach. The amount of gas controls the fish's buoyancy to keep it at the right level in the water. It can add more gas to go up, or lose gas to go down.

What is matter?

Matter is everything around you! It has three states: a solid, a liquid, or a gas.

Why does ice cream melt?

Materials change state as they heat up or cool down. Heating a solid above its melting point turns it to liquid. The melting point for ice cream is 0° Celsius.

How does a liquid become a gas?

Heating a liquid to its boiling point turns it to a gas. The boiling point of water is 100° Celsius.

Melting and boiling are reversible. If you cool a gas below its boiling point it becomes liquid again. And if you cool a liquid below its melting point it becomes solid.

Not all things melt when heated – some just burn. Which of these things do you think would melt?

- Woolly sweater
- Egg
- Glass bottle
- Sausage
- Toffee
- Metal key
- Book
- Wooden chair

Answer: glass, toffee and metal melt

A compendium of questions

Why is it cold at the North and South Poles?

The Earth is like a ball, so the top and bottom don't get much direct sunlight as they face away from the Sun.

Where do stars go in the daytime?

Nowhere! The light from the Sun is so bright that they just don't show up in daytime.

Why does the tide go in and out?

The Moon's gravity pulls on the oceans. As the Earth turns, the water is pulled one way and then the other.

What is a cloud made of?

Tiny drops of water, so light that they are held up by the air. If too much water collects, the drops get heavier and fall as rain.

Why do I burp?

Food breaking down in your stomach makes gases. This collects in bubbles which come out at your top or bottom!

At the South Pole, which way is up?

Towards the sky. Down is always towards the centre of the Earth. There is no up or down in space.

Could astronauts go to the Sun?

No – the Sun is far too hot for any person or spaceship to survive getting close to.

Why does a balloon go bang?

The air inside is under a lot of pressure. When the balloon bursts, air rushes out in a fast-moving wave. We hear this as a bang.

Why isn't the world covered in poo?

Poo is eaten and broken down by dung beetles, worms and micro organisms. So poo is food for some things!

Why don't I freeze solid in icy weather?

You're warm-blooded, which means your body uses energy to keep you at a safe temperature.

Is a bubble a solid, liquid or gas?

It is gas with a very thin skin of liquid around it.

Can I be a scientist when I grow up?

Yes! Anyone can be a scientist – just stay curious!